WAR, PEACE, AND THE BIBLE

Study by Vaughn CroweTipton
Commentary by Brett Younger

Free downloadable Teaching Guide for this study available at
NextSunday.com/teachingguides

NextSunday Resources
6316 Peake Road
Macon, Georgia 31210-3960
1-800-747-3016
©2015 by NextSunday Resources
All rights reserved.

TABLE OF CONTENTS

War, Peace, and the Bible

Study Introduction 1

Lesson 1 Defending the Homeland
1 Samuel 30:1-4, 11-20
Study 3
Commentary 11

Lesson 2 Submitting to Authority
Romans 13:1-7
Study 19
Commentary 27

Lesson 3 Longing for Peace
Isaiah 2:1-4
Study 35
Commentary 43

Lesson 4 Turning the Other Cheek
Luke 6:27-36
Study 51
Commentary 59

HOW TO USE THIS STUDY

NextSunday Resources Adult Bible Studies are designed to help adults study Scripture seriously within the context of the larger Christian tradition and, through that process, find their faith renewed, challenged, and strengthened. We study the Scriptures because we believe they affect our current lives in important ways. Each study contains the following three components:

Study Guide

Each study guide lesson is arranged in four movements:

Reflecting recalls a contemporary story, anecdote, example, or illustration to help us anticipate the session's relevance in our lives.

Studying is centered on giving the biblical material in-depth attention while often surrounding it with helpful insights from theology, ethics, church history, and other areas.

Understanding helps us find relevant connections between our lives and the biblical message.

What About Me? provides brief statements that help unite life issues with the meaning of the biblical text.

Commentary

Each study guide lesson is accompanied by an additional, in-depth commentary on the biblical material. Written by a different author than the study guide, each commentary gives the opportunity for learners to approach the Scripture text from a separate but complementary viewpoint.

Teaching Guide

In addition to the provided study guide and commentary, *NextSunday Resources* also provides a *free* downloadable teaching guide, available at NextSunday.com. Each teaching guide gives the teacher tools for focusing on the content of each study guide lesson through additional commentary and Bible background information. Through teacher helps and teaching options, each teaching guide also provides substance for variety and choice in the preparation of each lesson.

NextSunday
Resources

STUDY INTRODUCTION

In the 1986 film, *The Mission*, Jeremy Irons and Robert De Niro play the central characters in a saga about the church, a mission, and a native people. Irons plays Father Gabriel, who is committed to nonviolence. De Niro plays Rodrigo Mendoza, a former warrior haunted by his sin and now a faithful follower of the Church. The film documents their tension-filled yet deep relationship. In the end, both have to make a decision as the mission where they live and work is scheduled for destruction and relocation. Father Gabriel chooses nonviolence to combat the forces of evil; Mendoza chooses to fight for the rights of the natives. Most of us don't need Hollywood to bring the issues of war and peace home for us. As people of faith, we are faced daily with our participation in violent actions, our willingness to allow violence in the world to continue, and our response to violence in our lives.

The Bible does not give us an easy answer. Sometimes we hear ancient Israel on its march through the promised land. Other times we hear Jesus unwilling to raise a hand against those who persecuted and ultimately killed him. There are days when we can side with the psalmist, who lashes out in anger against his enemies. Other times, we know Jesus was right that we should not return violence for violence, that we must pray for our enemies, and that we must love even those who do not love us. How can we do these things? Is there a place for war and violence in our faith?

As you read, study, and contemplate these sessions, take time to look deeply within yourself. Although it is difficult, self-examination can enable our learning and activate our engagement with the world and our faith.

DEFENDING
THE HOMELAND

1 Samual 30:1-4, 11-20

Central Question

When is it acceptable to fight?

Scripture

1 Samuel 30:1-4, 11-20 1 Now when David and his men came to Ziklag on the third day, the Amalekites had made a raid on the Negeb and on Ziklag. They had attacked Ziklag, burned it down, 2 and taken captive the women and all who were in it, both small and great; they killed none of them, but carried them off, and went their way. 3 When David and his men came to the city, they found it burned down, and their wives and sons and daughters taken captive. 4 Then David and the people who were with him raised their voices and wept, until they had no more strength to weep.... 11 In the open country they found an Egyptian, and brought him to David. They gave him bread and he ate, they gave him water to drink; 12 they also gave him a piece of fig cake and two clusters of raisins. When he had eaten, his spirit revived; for he had not eaten bread or drunk water for three days and three nights. 13 Then David said to him, "To whom do you belong? Where are you from?" He said, "I am a young man of Egypt, servant to an Amalekite. My master left me behind because I fell sick three days ago. 14 We had made a raid on the Negeb of the Cherethites and on that which belongs to Judah and on the Negeb of Caleb; and we burned Ziklag down." 15 David said to him, "Will you take me down to this raiding party?" He said, "Swear to me by God that you will not kill me, or hand me over to my master, and I will take you down to them." 16 When he had taken him down, they were spread out all over the ground, eating and drinking and dancing, because of the great amount of spoil they had taken from the land of the Philistines and from the land of Judah. 17 David attacked them from twilight until the evening of the next day. Not one of them escaped, except four hundred young men, who mounted camels and fled. 18 David recovered all that the Amalekites had taken; and David rescued his two wives. 19 Nothing was missing, whether small or great, sons or daughters, spoil or anything that had been taken; David brought back everything. 20 David also captured all the flocks and herds, which were driven ahead of the other cattle; people said, "This is David's spoil."

Reflecting

Like many kids, I endured my share of bullying. I have no idea why bullies targeted me. I just know that it was an awful experience. The truth is that I was big for my age. Maybe my size roused aggression in my peers. Whatever the reason, my parents dealt with an upset child at least once a week when I got into yet another fight on the way home from school. I hated fighting, so what happened often felt close to domestic terrorism. Kids called me names, pushed me, kicked me, stole items from me, and hit me. One day, a gang of kids attacked and beat me. I can remember them laughing as they hit me. I came home that afternoon screaming and crying. I wanted it to stop, and I was angry. My dad had finally seen enough. He handed me a baseball bat and told me to go back out there and take care of business. Before you think badly of my father, remember he too was tired of the abuse. We had been to the school. We had talked with parents. We had tried everything. Dad was telling me it was time to fight back.

> To what extremes would you go to protect your loved ones?

Do we ever reach a point when it is acceptable to fight? Maybe you read my story above and thought I waited too long to fight back. Or maybe you read it and questioned my father's wisdom and why he would encourage a kid to use a baseball bat to end violence. The reality, however, is that all of us must choose our responses both individually and corporately. For people of faith, the Bible and our discernment as Christians can provide a compass to direct our thinking. Our struggle is that the Bible never simply says, "Do it like this...." Instead, we get stories and teachings that are open to interpretation and debate. It's no wonder Christians disagree on the use of violence in war, conflict, or our personal lives. How can we know if and when it is acceptable to fight?

Studying

This biblical story from Samuel focuses on David and the Amalekites. For most of us, David is a familiar character. The Amalekites are another story. Historically, they are the descendents of Esau and one of ancient Israel's traditional enemies. Since there is no evidence of the Amalekites beyond the Bible, all we know about them comes from within the biblical story itself. The first encounter between this group and ancient Israel was an attack recorded in Exodus 17:8-13. In this instance, it is unclear why Amalekites attacked. Likely, it related to Israelite encroachment into traditional Amalekite territory. In a later description of this attack (Deut 25:17-18), the Amalekites are described as being especially cruel, and a ban, or declaration, is placed on them. It is a call to "blot out the remembrance of Amalek from under heaven" (Deut 25:19). In one of Balaam's prophetic speeches, he offers what may be the only good word in the Bible about the Amalekites, but he follows it with a declaration that they will "perish forever."

It is important to recognize that Israel was both a nation and a people of Yahweh its God. As a nation, it lived among other nations and was subject to the struggles—military, economic, social, and political—that are common to all nations. As a people of God, they Israelites were constantly being reminded that they were to put their trust in the Lord (cf. Ps. 20.7). (LaSor, 791)

David's encounter with the Amalekites actually begins much earlier and relates to his conflict with Saul. Saul's kingship in Israel has deteriorated, and now he wishes to destroy his rival,

David. In order to escape Saul, David ventures with his troops into Philistine territory. Although it stopped Saul, this move was risky for David. If the people identified David as siding with the Philistines, his reputation would falter. David seems unafraid to take risks, even at this level. He bargains with the Philistine leaders and secures the city of Ziklag as a home base (27:5-7). Operating from Ziklag, David acts as a raider against the cities to the south—Philistine cities (27:8). In the process, David kills everyone in his path (27:9).

When the Philistine leader, Achish—who agreed to allow David to live and work in his territory in return for his loyalty (27:5-7)—asks David about the raids, David lies. He says his raids are against Saul and his people, against Judah and its allies. Of course, David is actually raiding the enemies of Judah—namely, other Philistine cities. In other words, David works a grand deception. Note that the cities David names in 27:10 are not the cities named in 27:8. By raiding Philistine cities and killing everyone in them (after all, dead men tell no tales), David leaves no one to implicate him. He hopes Achish will believe Saul raided the Philistine cities and choose to help David by pursuing Saul. All the while, David will ensure his place in Israel by selectively destroying the Philistines internally. This prehistory to our text is not pretty. It portrays David as ruthless and calculating.

Achish trusts David. David appears to have severed his relationship with Israel. Achish decides to make his new friend, the "former Israelite," his own bodyguard (28:2). The problem is that Achish now wants David to go with him to fight Saul. David cannot afford the revelation of his deception among the Philistines *or* the Israelites. If the Philistines find out, they will kill him. If Israel finds out, they will turn their favor toward Saul.

Fortunately for David, the commanders of the Philistine army do not share Achish's enthusiasm for David and demand that he return to Ziklag rather than going into battle (29:4-8). David plays his part well, appearing hurt by the mistrust, but this turn of events is the break he needs. It appears that the only trustworthy characters in this story are the Philistine commanders. David plays Achish for the fool. Achish lives up to that role. David tricks everyone except the commanders. In fact, Achish's apology

(29:8-11) serves as a dark irony. His trust in David is completely misplaced.

Upon his return to Ziklag, David finds that his ruse has been discovered. One of the cities he raided in this deception was an Amalekite city. On that raid, as with many others, David killed everyone, taking all the livestock and any other bounty he could find. Now, the Amalekites have returned the favor (30:1). There is, however, a difference. While David killed everyone in the Amalekite city, the Amalekite attackers killed no one in their raid on Ziklag. The women and children of David's army, even his own two wives, are now captives. His followers see the downside of David's behavior, which brought this calamity upon them. They are ready to stone him. David, on the other hand, finds strength in his relationship with God (30:6). This statement is striking, for David's actions throughout these events seem out of step with God. He is portrayed as an interesting mix of faithful follower and manipulative rascal.

David follows the Amalekites and successfully rescues the women and children of his camp. David again kills everyone except a few young men who escape on camels. It appears that David is actually more bloodthirsty than the Amalekites; remember, "they killed no one" (30:2). At the same time, we must realize that these stories are not written as history and thus are not evenhanded. Instead, they promote Israel as a people. In the Israelites' minds, the long history between them and the Amalekites transcended this one event. Basically, the Israelites believed their enemies had it coming. In that sense, David "saved" Israel from the Amalekites when their present king, Saul, would not. Despite the inconsistencies in David's character, the story is about Saul's downfall and David's rise. In the process, we catch an inside glimpse of the messiness of international relationships in the ancient world. This text raises more questions than it answers.

Understanding

This text is harsh in many respects. It portrays David in a negative light and shows the Amalekites as Israel's enemy but also as being pushed toward violent revenge, and it details the manipulation of the Philistines to achieve a "good" goal. For us to learn from this story, we have to address several issues.

First, is it ever acceptable to lie in order to do good? David's deception helped Israel in the long run. Saul's bankrupt reign was nearly over, and the danger of the Philistines and Amalekites was real. David was already assuming the kingship through his leadership and ability to handle, even if with questionable tactics, Israel's enemies. The text never critiques David, never questions his behavior, and never points to other options. We can read this overt acceptance of David as normative, as a call to follow our leaders in the same way, but we don't have to. It may be that the writer of Samuel offered these stories as an insider to Israel's history, intending only to show that David was the new leader to replace Saul.

Second, when is fighting acceptable? In this story, a first glance indicates that David had every right to track down the Amalekites and save his abducted followers. If our reading of the story includes only chapter 30, then the attack appears unprovoked. The truth, however, is larger. David's earlier behavior and actions toward the Amalekites instigated the raid of Ziklag. While his actions did not validate the raid, they brought it about as a retaliatory move from an old enemy. Sadly, David's disregard for life in the earlier chapters of Samuel brings about more killing in the latter chapters of Samuel.

According to an old Jewish tradition, God's angels began to chant in jubilation once all of ancient Israel finally crossed the Red Sea and the waters drowned the forces of Egypt. That angelic song, however, was cut short by the voice of God, who questioned, "The work of my hands has drowned in the sea and you chant songs?" Apparently, according to the ancient rabbis, God

> No matter how well we do the work of just peacemaking, not all conflicts will be resolved. Some conflicts will lead to war, or the brink of war. We will need to debate whether to make war, and, if the political processes produce war, we will need to debate whether we ourselves should support or oppose it, participate in it or resist it. We will still need a theology of the restraint of war—*either pacifism or just war theory*. (Stassen, 231)

does not "rejoice in the downfall of the wicked" (b. Meg 10b; b. San 39b). Even the cruel Egyptians of the Exodus story are God's own creation, God's own children. Jesus later argues the same point, saying, "Love your enemies...turn the other cheek... blessed are the peacemakers." David had yet to learn that truth. The question is, have we learned it? In our lives and the world at large, the answers to these issues may depend on the particular circumstances. However, we must never lose sight of the way of Jesus.

What About Me?

• *Is it acceptable to protect myself and my family?* In a day and age when violence is part of our everyday lives, this is a fair question. The struggle is not only with the answer, however; it is with our assumptions. Too often we wait until the fight starts to think of what to do. We react rather than behaving proactively. Jesus gives us no clear answer on when or if we can fight, but he is clear that we should make peace, love our enemies, and pray for those who are against us. Perhaps we should start there.

• *Why does the Bible not answer our questions?* Many times, the Bible doesn't address our direct questions and specific issues. We need to remember that the biblical books were not written to answer our tough questions. They were written to tell us how our spiritual ancestors lived out their faith. The Bible tells us their story in relationship to God. Our stories are not yet written, and while we can learn much from our ancestors' stories, we also must choose our paths based on how God calls us today.

• *Why is the Old Testament so violent?* The wars and battles of the Old Testament led some in the early history of the church to think that the Old Testament God and the New Testament God were not the same God. However, many Old Testament texts call for peace. Violence was as much, if not more, a part of that culture as it is of our own. Rather than shielding us from those conflicts, the biblical writers show us their struggles and their faith all at the same time.

Resources

William Sanford LaSor, "War," *The Oxford Companion to the Bible*, ed. Bruce M. Metzger and Michael D. Coogan (New York: Oxford University Press, 1993).

Glen H. Stassen, *Just Peacemaking* (Louisville: Westminster/John Knox, 1992).

DEFENDING
THE HOMELAND
1 Samual 30:1-4, 11-20

Introduction

War has taken a heavy toll on humanity. The total number of
people killed in wars is staggering, but people still make war. It
seems that we would learn from the horrors and tragedies of past
wars, but that is not the case. Tragically, more people were killed
in wars in the twentieth century than in the preceding ten thou-
sand years combined! The century-by-century casualty
breakdown looks like this:

1500s – 1.6 million killed
1600s – 6.1 million killed
1700s – 7 million killed
1800s – 19.4 million killed
1900s – 109 million killed (Walter Wink, *The Powers that Be* [New
York: Doubleday, 1998] 137)

With statistics like these, we can only shudder to think what the
number will be for the 2000s.

This unit of study focuses on the issue of war and peace and,
in particular, what Scripture says about it. Over the next four
weeks, we will study two Old Testament passages and two New
Testament passages and wrestle with what the Bible says about
war and peace.

This Sunday's passage from 1 Samuel 30 tells of an incident
in the life of David. The Amalekites had attacked his people,
taking some away as hostages. David didn't hesitate to give chase,
apprehend the Amalekites, and exact a sure and certain punishment. The story is filled with mayhem, death, and revenge. David
also took as his spoil the flocks and herds of the Amalekites. Not

surprisingly, David returned from that encounter a conquering hero.

But the story raises a host of questions: When is it acceptable to fight? Are God's people supposed to kill, pillage, and steal? Is someone who does what David did a hero or a criminal? Finally, how does this story match up with the life and teachings of Jesus? In this story, we face the thorny issues of war and peace and consider questions that yield no easy answers.

Christians have struggled for centuries with stories like this one in 1 Samuel 30, and three distinct philosophies about war have developed—holy war, just war, and no war. Knowing these three philosophies and how Christians have reasoned about war in the past can help us sort through our own beliefs about war and peace.

Holy War

One thing is certain: the Bible—especially the Old Testament—contains many stories of war. It is filled with violent confrontations, many of them sanctioned by God. Walter Wink writes,

> The violence of the Old Testament has always been a scandal to Christianity. The church has usually ducked the issue, either by allegorizing the Old Testament or by rejecting it. Biblical scholar Raymond Schwager points out that there are six hundred passages of explicit violence in the Hebrew Bible, one thousand verses where God's own violent actions of punishment are described, a hundred passages where Yahweh expressly commands others to kill people, and several stories where God irrationally kills or tries to kill for no apparent reason (for example, Exod. 4:24-26). Violence, Schwager concludes, is easily the most often mentioned activity in the Hebrew Bible. (84)

It is not surprising, then, that some Christians throughout history have adopted the philosophy of holy war, war that is ordained by God and fought for divine purposes. When the Crusaders went to battle in 1095, for example, they were convinced that God was on their side and that they did God's will in liberating Christian pilgrimage sites in the Holy Land from

Muslim control—even if it meant exterminating their Muslim enemies. Soldiers in a holy war believe God is on their side and victory is certain.

Just War

In the fifth century, Augustine proposed the just war theory, an approach that has been a popular philosophy among Christians ever since. This philosophy says that God doesn't sanction war; that, in fact, God is opposed to war. But it also allows for certain situations when war is justified because the alternatives are even worse. According to the just war theory, when innocent people are tyrannized by evil, it is time to draw swords or drop bombs. War is not good, but sometimes it is the lesser of two evils.

Just war proponents typically consider a war justified if the following conditions are met:

(1) The war must have a *just cause.*
(2) It must be waged by a *legitimate authority.*
(3) It must be *formally declared.*
(4) It must be fought with a *peaceful intention.*
(5) It must be a *last resort.*
(6) There must be reasonable *hope of success.*
(7) The means used must possess *proportionality* to the end sought.
(8) *Noncombatants* must be given immunity.
(9) *Prisoners* must be treated humanely.
(10) *International treaties and conventions* must be honored.
    (Wink, 132–33)

If these conditions are met, just war proponents say war can be waged and can even be the will of God.

No War

In her book, *A People's History of Christianity* (New York: HarperCollins, 2009), Diana Butler Bass writes,

> Before theologians Ambrose and Augustine in later decades made a case for just war, Christians were not allowed to fight.

No record exists that Christians served in the Roman army before the year 170. The strong consensus of the early church teachers was that war meant killing, killing was murder, and murder was wrong.... Justin Martyr, Irenaeus, Hippolytus, Tertullian, and Origen all specifically condemned participation in war. (71)

Ever since those early Christians took a stand against war of any kind, some believers have resolutely refused to participate in any military conflict, no matter how seemingly just the cause. They have said that Jesus is the Prince of Peace and that his people must be peacemakers. They advocate peaceful resistance against evil oppressors but refuse to take up arms and fight. The "no war" advocates believe that retaliation only perpetuates conflict. They take seriously Jesus' command to turn the other cheek and to love one's enemies.

Drawing Tentative Conclusions

In light of these different views, let's try to draw tentative conclusions about the issue of war and peace.

First, *Christians disagree on the issue*. It's possible that in your class, you'll have proponents of all three views. Some will see God as a warring deity, intent on stamping out evil however and wherever possible. Others will be just war advocates and see war as a regrettably necessary deterrent to tyranny. Others will believe that Christians must never return evil for evil and will stand alongside those who refuse to take up arms. The first two groups will have no trouble with David's military victory in 1 Samuel 30; the third group will see this story as an example of brutality from an era before Jesus taught his message of nonviolence.

Second, *the biblical story moves and develops*. Place some of those Old Testament passages about God demanding the slaughter of Israel's enemies alongside Jesus' commands to love one's enemies and turn the other cheek, and you'll see that Scripture does not speak with a unified voice on these issues. The Bible is a dynamic document. Its thought grows and develops over time.

Third, *we must be discerning and intelligent interpreters of Scripture*. Because the Bible moves and grows, we must never pull something out of the Old Testament to make it applicable for today simply because it's in the Bible. We could pull verses out of certain parts of the Old Testament that would allow us to stone our disobedient children, practice polygamy, denigrate women, retaliate against anyone who offends us, and solve all our disputes with violence. Wise biblical interpreters know the Bible moves, and they try to move with it.

Fourth, *Jesus is the best revelation of God we have*. The New Testament tells us that Jesus was the exact image of God. If we want to know about the character of God, all we have to do is look at Jesus. That idea helps us as we try to interpret the Bible. Anything in the Bible that contradicts the life and witness of Jesus is insufficient. Jesus is the plumb line by which we measure biblical truth. If we must choose between slaughtering our enemies, as some Old Testament passages advocate, or loving our enemies, as Jesus advocates, we should always go with Jesus.

Fifth, *God is a God of peace*. Because Jesus is our best revelation of God, we can be sure that God desires reconciliation, forgiveness, and grace. God was in Christ, reconciling the world to himself, and now he has committed unto us the ministry of reconciliation (2 Cor 5:19). God breaks down divisive walls, and we are to break down those walls too. If we are to believe and follow Jesus, we must make peacemaking a crucial part of our discipleship.

Sixth, *the issue of war and peace begins with me*. Ultimately, it is not only about international relations. It's about *my* marriage, *my* church, *my* job, and *my* relationships. When Jesus talked about loving our enemies and turning the other cheek, he wasn't addressing political leaders. He was addressing ordinary people who needed to become peacemakers where they lived, worked, and worshiped.

Conclusion

Nathaniel Hawthorne wrote a short story titled "The Great Stone Face." It is the story of a young man named Ernest who is enamored with a face carved on the side of mountain. Day after day, Ernest stares at this stone face. By the end of the story, his human face has started to resemble the one on the mountain.

Remarkably, he has been transformed into the image of the face at which he has gazed.

The truth in that story is irrefutable: What captures our attention shapes us. Focus day after day on a particular person or thing, and it will transform you. Nowhere is that more true than in our concept of God. We become like the God we worship. We are each transformed into the face of the God at which we gaze. Certainly, our concept of God will affect our view of war and peace.

If our God is a warring God, the God of the Old Testament who regularly issues declarations of war on Israel's enemies, that God will shape us. We will have no problem with any "holy war" that endeavors to stamp out evil and bring in God's kingdom.

If our God is a God who favors war over tyranny and oppression and can use war to bring about good, that God will shape us. We will have no problem with a "just war" that protects the innocent and seeks to alleviate atrocities

If our God is a God who hates war and really means we are to love our enemies and turn the other cheek when someone attacks us, that God will shape us, too. We will have a problem with any war and will see it as an inadequate, un-Christian response to evil.

As always happens, our view of God affects the rest of our lives. In this case, it determines our view of war and peace. And our view of war and peace lets everyone know what kind of God we serve.

If nothing else, these lessons on war and peace will give us occasion to consider again our own concept of God.

Notes

Notes

SUBMITTING TO AUTHORITY

Romans 13:1-7

Central Question

What are the tensions between my discipleship and my citizenship?

Scripture

Romans 13:1-7 1 Let every person be subject to the governing authorities; for there is no authority except from God, and those authorities that exist have been instituted by God. 2 Therefore whoever resists authority resists what God has appointed, and those who resist will incur judgment. 3 For rulers are not a terror to good conduct, but to bad. Do you wish to have no fear of the authority? Then do what is good, and you will receive its approval; 4 for it is God's servant for your good. But if you do what is wrong, you should be afraid, for the authority does not bear the sword in vain! It is the servant of God to execute wrath on the wrongdoer. 5 Therefore one must be subject, not only because of wrath but also because of conscience. 6 For the same reason you also pay taxes, for the authorities are God's servants, busy with this very thing. 7 Pay to all what is due them—taxes to whom taxes are due, revenue to whom revenue is due, respect to whom respect is due, honor to whom honor is due.

Reflecting

Unless you read Latin, have seen the movie *National Treasure*, or are a history buff, you may not know the phrase. *Annuit coeptis* is one of the three national mottos proposed by the designers of our Constitution: Franklin, Jefferson, and Adams. Of course, the motto we know best is *e pluribus unum* ("Out of many, one"). You will find it on American currency and coins. But *annuit coeptis* is there too. On the back of the dollar bill, right above the pyramid with the floating eyeball, you see the Latin

> Listen, O kings, and understand; learn, O judges of the ends of the earth. Give ear, you that rule over multitudes, and boast of many nations. For your dominion was given you from the Lord, and your sovereignty from the Most High; he will search out your works and inquire into your plans. (Wisdom of Solomon 6:1-3)

annuit coeptis. It means, "Providence has favored us." Don't bother looking for it in your Bible, and you should note that it doesn't say, "*God* has favored us." The phrase, from the ancient classical writer Virgil, was an attempt both to acknowledge the enormity of creating this new nation and to avoid the mixing of church and state. The pyramid points to the mighty undertaking of building this country. The eye signals that forces greater than ourselves are at work. The phrase *annuit coeptis* allows people to interpret "providence" however they see fit. The designers of our country, many of them Baptists like John Leland and Roger Williams or other sorts of Christians, knew that separation of church and state was essential for this new nation. This means that, while the two can certainly speak to one another, one should never coerce or tell the other what to do or believe.

In fact, the Bible addresses our allegiance to the state, to the country, and to our leaders. Paul says in Romans 12:2, "Don't be conformed to this age." First Peter 2:13 says, "Be subject, for the Lord's sake, to every human institution whether it be to the emperor as supreme or to governors as sent by God." On the other hand, Revelation 13 clearly indicates that the ruling authorities are sometimes against the people of God and work to their detriment. Should Christians conform? Should they be wary? The book of Acts describes the apostles willfully breaking the law (Acts 4:1-4, 19-20) and not submitting to the authorities. In fact, Paul and Peter both escaped jail by the hand of God.

What are we to do today? How do we reconcile our relationship to God with our relationship to our country?

Studying

Depending on the date you assume, Paul wrote Romans either at the end of emperor Claudius's reign (AD 41–54) or at the beginning of Nero's reign (AD 54–68). Nero is the more likely of the two. A tyrant, Nero is known for his open persecution of Christians, the execution of his own mother (and many others close to him), and the great fire of Rome, which he ultimately blamed on Christians. In this climate, Paul wrote to a group of small house churches in the city of Rome. His letter has several goals, one of which is to stabilize these communities of faith in the face of oncoming oppression and persecution.

In the world of Paul and Jesus—a Roman world guided by Roman values—how people lived out their honor mattered. In that culture, honor was a limited commodity, like money, that dictated one's place in society. Showing dishonor to those in authority was similar to treason. Rome had no patience for individuals or groups that criticized the status quo.

> [Paul] reminded them to respect civil authority as a basis for law and order and to deal responsibly with issues such as taxes much in the way that Jesus argued (13:1-7; cf. Mark 12:7). (Borchert, 774)

Also, their culture was social in nature, not individualistic like ours. We make our choices based on our wants and needs. In the ancient world, the group mattered, not the individual. People made choices for the good of the group. Reward and punishment happened not to the individual, but to the group. "Guilt by association" would have been a commonly accepted axiom in that context.

These ideas matter because we cannot read Paul's letter as if it were written in our context. How the Roman churches understood themselves and their relationship to the governing authorities in the middle of the first century differs vastly from our understanding of church and government today.

In the ancient world, Paul knew that if even a few members of the Roman churches dishonored the emperor, the entire Christian community would be deemed guilty. Therefore, in this letter, Paul calls the Roman churches to live honorably with the emperor and the empire because of where they are and because he

sees the potential for impending persecution. He understands the pressure and violence the government can bring upon the lives of these early Christians. Rather than encouraging them to rebel, he asks them to live peaceably within the system.

In wrestling with this passage, Christians have pondered whether Paul's charge to submit to the governing authorities is a moral absolute. For example, was the Confessing Church of Germany wrong to defy Adolf Hitler and the Nazis openly? Following the logic of Romans 13, shouldn't they have "stayed out of politics" and sought to live as loyal citizens of the Third Reich? What about Christians in apartheid-era South Africa? What about Christians in North America who have moral concerns about certain political aspects? What does it mean to "be subject" to the government's officers, and is there no room for peaceful resistance against a government at odds with the values of God's kingdom?

Why did Paul *not* ask the Christians in Rome to trust God and stand up in faith for what they believed? The reason is fairly simple: Paul's advice to the Roman believers was tailored to their particular situation in light of Paul's end-times expectations. Early in his ministry, Paul believed Jesus would return in his own lifetime. Later in his ministry, Paul revised this belief and recognized that his churches might have to survive under pressure for many years to come. In Romans, however, we see a different approach than either of these. At this time, Paul asks the church to endure their current pressures because he believes they will end soon. We must read Paul's instruction in this light.

This is not the only place where Paul gives advice based on specific historical or cultural factors. Several times in 1 Corinthians, for example, he makes clear that his words are merely his personal advice and not a binding command from God (7:6, 12, 25; 9:3). Furthermore, while it is difficult for us to grasp or admit, we may at times disagree with Paul's advice.

> Other than civil government, to what other authorities are Christians subject? When is it time to ask whether these authorities should be resisted?

How do we know when Paul was offering his personal opinion rather than a "word from God"? How do we know when it is acceptable to reach conclusions different from those of the Apostle? We should always discern these places in Scripture with care, keeping the rest of Scripture in mind.

For example, because of Paul's words, many Christians once believed that slavery was not only acceptable but God's command. Other Christians disagreed and took what Paul said about slaves obeying their masters (Eph 6:5; Col 3:22) as either advice or as a cultural issue not relevant for our day.

We should not be overly concerned in these instances. Even the Bible does not always agree with itself. While Paul says, "Honor (be subject to) the authorities," Jesus himself stood against the authorities in his time. Revelation 13 also reveals a scenario in which Christians are to stand against the authorities. Acts 4 shows Peter and John disobeying the authorities. Paul himself lands in jail on numerous occasions for his civil disobedience, and on at least one occasion he refused to be released until the city magistrates came personally to offer a public apology for his false imprisonment (Acts 16:35-40).

Paul's words in Romans 13 are meant for a first-century Roman audience. Still, we can learn from them. Surely, for example, all would agree that there are occasions when looking out for the good of the community may override the needs of individuals. At the same time, in many instances Christian discipleship calls us to stand against the authorities for reasons of love, justice, or community. We must strive to discern the most Christlike way to act in each situation.

Understanding

It may be that in instances where we must decide between our discipleship and our citizenship, we should do what Jesus once suggested. When asked about paying taxes to the emperor, Jesus responded that we should give to the government what belongs to the government and give to God what belongs to God (Mk 12:13-17). Deciding which is which is not always easy, however, and I feel sure Jesus knew that when he said these words. We are not always clear on what belongs to the government. Good people disagree. At the same time, what does *not* belong to God?

There is no question that Christians experience conflicts of loyalty when the claims of the state demand a level of allegiance we owe to God alone. Again, Jesus reminds us that at the end of the day, we can only serve one master (Mt 6:24). For Christians, this demand sometimes puts us in a difficult spot. Some who do not share our faith may never truly understand why we help the poor, why we insist on justice for the oppressed, why we continuously side with the outcast. We do not do these things because they are merely the advice of a wise spiritual counselor, and they certainly do not help us in relating to difficult leaders. They are not easy steps to take, and they do not always help us feel better about ourselves. They are, however, the essence of God's all-inclusive gospel of grace.

There will be times—as in the Gospels, as in Acts, and as in Revelation—when Christians will have to stand against leaders, against those in positions of authority. Choosing when and how to do so is a matter of prayer, conscience, and discernment. Sometimes we are fortunate enough to have leaders who listen to God and act fairly for all, but not always.

What About Me?

• *What do I do when I disagree with portions of the Bible?* Disagreement is difficult, especially when we disagree with those we love, those we trust, or those who shape our faith. At the same time, the Bible fortunately gives us many experiences and voices so that we can, as Paul says, "work out our salvation with fear and trembling." Part of that work is discerning which parts of Scripture are bound to a particular time and circumstance and which parts give timeless instructions to all Christ's followers.

• *How do I know when I should disagree with someone in authority?* Disagreement is often viewed negatively. However, when handled well, disagreement often breeds better ideas, new perceptions, and rich openness that allows us to hear one another and benefit from one another's ideas. It also means that as individuals, we must practice the skills of discernment the same way we practice anything we want to do better. Learning to discern our personal motives, God's call, and the places where we disagree is paramount in all relationships.

• *What if my community disagrees with me?* None of us like to stand alone. It is one of the hardest things to do. Anytime we find ourselves as the lone dissenter, we are wise to ponder what we hear from our community. Self-evaluation is not easy, but it is essential. Sometimes we find that we need to listen to our community and adapt. Other times, we bear the difficult burden of standing alone for what we believe is true.

Resources

Gerald L. Borchert, "Romans, Letter to the," *Mercer Dictionary of the Bible*, ed. Watson E. Mills et al. (Macon GA: Mercer University Press, 1990)

SUBMITTING
TO AUTHORITY
Romans 13:1-7

Introduction

Are Christians obligated to support government officials and their policies even when those officials and policies are evil? Does the Bible command blind obedience to government authorities?

In the 1930s and early 1940s, many German Christians believed that to be the case. They read Romans 13:1-7 and interpreted it to mean they owed allegiance to Adolph Hitler even through his regime was rife with violence and atrocity. For further support, they cited Martin Luther's interpretation of that passage: "Christians should not refuse, under the pretext of religion, to obey men, especially evil ones" (Martin Luther, *Lectures on Romans* [Philadelphia: Westminster, 1961] 358). Those German Christians read Romans 13 and grudgingly decided that they owed Hitler their support.

In today's lesson, we put these verses under the microscope and consider what it means to be subject to governing authorities. Is Luther's interpretation valid? Does this passage demand blind obedience to the powers that be? Are we obligated, as Christians, to support our government even when we disagree with it?

As we look at Romans 13:1-7, we will use the following outline. First, we will consider *the mandate*. In verse 1, Paul says we are to be subject to the government authorities because God instituted them.

Second, we will look at *the rationale* in verses 2-5. In those verses, Paul lays out the reasons for the mandate to obey the government.

Third, we will probe *the implications* in verses 6-7. In those final two verses, Paul shows how obedience to the authorities manifests itself in practical action.

By the time we get to the end of the passage, we should have a clearer idea of what Paul said about submitting to government leaders and begin to make applications to our own citizenship.

The Mandate

Paul's advice to obey government leaders might come as a surprise. After all, in the preceding chapter of Romans, Paul implores his readers not to be "conformed to this world, but... transformed by the renewing of your minds" (Rom 12:2). At the beginning of Romans 12, it sounds like Paul is getting ready to launch a manifesto of resistance and nonconformity.

In that light, Romans 13 seems shocking. This chapter begins, "Let every person be subject to the government authorities; for there is no authority except from God, and those authorities that exist have been instituted by God" (v. 1). Whatever happened to Paul, the nonconformist and Christian rebel? Why this sudden shift of attitude?

As you read Paul's other correspondence, though, you realize this is not a shift at all. He consistently said the same thing in other letters. To Timothy he wrote,

> First of all, then, I urge that supplications, prayers, intercessions, and thanksgivings be made for everyone, for kings and all who are in high positions, so that we may lead a quiet and peaceable life in all godliness and dignity. (1 Tim 1:1-2)

(See also Titus 3:1-2). Paul consistently advocated obedience to the state.

Some scholars have suggested that Paul had practical reasons for advocating this obedience. William Barclay writes,

> In Paul's case, there was one immediate cause of his stressing civil obedience. The Jews were notoriously rebellious. Palestine, and especially Galilee, was constantly seething with insurrection. Above all there were the Zealots; they were convinced that there was no king for the Jews but God; and that no tribute

must be paid to anyone except God. (William Barclay, *The Letter to the Romans* [Philadelphia: Westminster, 1955] 187)

The Zealots were first-century terrorists who wrecked houses, burned crops, and assassinated fellow Jews who were too friendly with the Roman government. In some parts of Galilee, that was normal behavior. So maybe Paul was a nonconformist! He saw no value in the conduct the Zealots espoused. In fact, this was the exact opposite of the way followers of Jesus should conduct themselves. When you see the Zealots in the backdrop of Romans 13:1, the verse makes a lot of sense.

Charles Talbert provides more context for this verse and says that other circumstances may have conditioned Paul's attitude as well. According to Talbert,

[Paul] would have known of Claudius's decree in AD 49 that expelled Jews and Jewish Christians from Rome because of disturbances in the synagogue.... He wanted no repeat of that. Priscilla and Aquila had only recently returned to Rome.... He and his readers were living in the early years of Nero's reign when[, surrounded by several capable advisors including the philosopher Seneca,] the young emperor behaved properly. There had been no persecutions of Christians in Rome to date. This led to a generally positive attitude toward imperial power. (Charles Talbert, *Romans*, Smyth & Helwys Bible Commentary [Macon GA: Smyth & Helwys, 2002] 296)

Add up those reasons, and you can see why Paul would want the Christians of Rome to obey their civil authorities. First, he rejected the violence of the Zealots. Second, he didn't want the Christians to be expelled once again, as they were during the reign of Claudius. Third, he wanted Priscilla and Aquila's ministry in Rome to prosper. Fourth, he certainly didn't want to give Nero reason to be upset.

Therefore, Paul told his readers to be subject to the government authorities and to see those authorities as placed in their positions by God. Paul's mandate to the early Christians was not to follow the Zealots into a life of violence but to follow Jesus into a life of love.

The Rationale

Paul doesn't mention any of those reasons, though, for advocating civil obedience. In verses 2-5, he simply states that the government serves a valid and essential purpose: "It is the servant of God to execute wrath on the wrongdoer" (13:4).

There are several obvious benefits of government. Government provides us with services we could not get on our own: water, electrical power, sewage, streets and freeways, transportation, communication, and many more. We probably wouldn't realize all our government does for us until we were without those services for a while!

But Paul zeroes in on another thing the government provides: security and protection from evil people. As Paul saw it, the Roman government, for all its flaws, was God's instrument to save the world from chaos. In the ideal world, people would follow the Jesus way and love one another, but in the real world, evil people run rampant and wreak havoc unless someone or something restrains them. For Paul, that someone or something was the government. It was ordained by God to keep evil people at bay so that others could lead peaceful lives.

Paul experienced this protection firsthand. Several times in Acts, Roman authorities rescue Paul from angry mobs (see Acts 16:37-39, 18:12-17, and 22:24-29 as examples). He had learned from his own experience that civil authorities provide order and restraint that protects innocent people. We should be in subjection to the government authorities because, in the plan of God, those authorities are God's agents for order and stability— whether they know it or not.

The Implications

Because the authorities are God's agents, followers of Jesus should be good citizens. According to Paul in verses 6-7, there are practical implications to this notion: Christians should pay their taxes and give tribute to whom tribute is due, fear to whom fear is due, and honor to whom honor is due. In a modern democracy, we could add to his list by saying Christians should honor government leaders by being involved in important issues, voting consistently, supporting worthy candidates, and in general living as if government matters—because it does!

But there is also the issue I raised at the beginning of my comments. At what point does *obedience* to the government become *disobedience* to God? Granted, we are to respect government and see it as a gift of God, but what about situations like Hitler's Germany? What do we do when *civic* responsibility conflicts with *spiritual* responsibility?

Perhaps we should review Paul's argument to this point. First, he says to be subject to the authorities because God ordained them. Second, he explains why: government provides people the indispensable service of protection and security. Without government, evil people and unjust persecution would swallow even the Christian movement. Third, the implications are obvious. Christians should pay their taxes, live as loyal subjects, and honor those in leadership positions.

We shouldn't miss, though, that Paul also makes plain what *government* is supposed to be and do. Government is supposed to be ordained of God. It is supposed to protect good people from bad people. It is supposed to be worthy of people's tribute and honor. So Romans 13:1-7 not only speaks about citizens; it also speaks about government leaders. It sets the bar high and tells us what government can, and should, be.

What happens if government itself becomes evil? What do Christians do when the authorities are not the kind Paul describes in this passage? Paul Achtemeier writes,

> If then a government claims for itself the kind of devotion proper only to God and demands of its subjects that they perform evil rather than good, and if it punishes those who disobey such demands to do evil, that government no longer functions as a servant of God and is therefore no longer to be obeyed as such. (*Romans*, Interpretation [Atlanta: John Knox, 1985] 205)

In short, when a government becomes evil, it no longer fits what Paul had in mind when he wrote Romans 13, and we shouldn't feel obligated to be in subjection to evil men— regardless of what Luther said.

This does not, of course, settle the matter for us. We still have to decide at what point the government crosses that line. We still have to determine at what point it moves from the ranks of God's servants to become one of God's enemies. We still have to recognize at exactly what point our civil obedience must become civil *disobedience*.

Conclusion

There is no doubt that the spirit of this passage is one of respect and appreciation for civil authorities. Government is a gift of God we should not take for granted. If we take Paul seriously, we cannot send demeaning e-mails about political leaders we don't like, brand all politicians as crooks, or ignore the laws and decisions our leaders make. If we take our stand with Paul, we pray for the government, respect its authorities, and perform the duties of good citizens.

True, the time may come when we are convinced the state has crossed the line and become God's enemy. Then, we must resist nonviolently and speak as clearly as possible the way of Jesus as we understand it. But any stones we throw at government officials must come from a stance of love and unity, not anger and divisiveness.

When Jesus was confronted with the God-and-state issue, he responded by saying, "Give to the emperor the things that are the emperor's, and to God the things that are God's" (Mk 12:17). That verse seems to say that the political realm is valid and worthy of respect, but the kingdom of God stands above any institution people might create.

We may salute the flag, but first and foremost we bow before God.

Notes

Notes

LONGING FOR PEACE

Isaiah 2:1-4

Central Question

What can I do to make the world more peaceful?

Scripture

Isaiah 2:1-4 1 The word that Isaiah son of Amoz saw concerning Judah and Jerusalem. 2 In days to come the mountain of the LORD's house shall be established as the highest of the mountains, and shall be raised above the hills; all the nations shall stream to it. 3 Many peoples shall come and say, "Come, let us go up to the mountain of the LORD, to the house of the God of Jacob; that he may teach us his ways and that we may walk in his paths." For out of Zion shall go forth instruction, and the word of the LORD from Jerusalem. 4 He shall judge between the nations, and shall arbitrate for many peoples; they shall beat their swords into plowshares, and their spears into pruning hooks; nation shall not lift up sword against nation, neither shall they learn war any more.

Reflecting

In his book *Engaging the Powers*, Walter Wink argues that our society now buys fully into what he calls the "myth of redemptive violence." This myth is built on the belief that violence can save us. It assumes that violence done in the name of "good" is redemptive. He points to the movies, even the cartoons, we watch as prime examples. In a typical movie, a "good guy" or "good gal" is mistreated in some way. This character is larger than life and possibly even superhuman, although at first it appears that he or she may die. In the end, however, the hero vanquishes the villain and restores order to chaos—at least until the sequel. Wink argues that this myth now fuels international conflict and has reached the status of a national spirituality.

Does a spirituality of violence exist in our culture and in our world? If so, what does it mean? Few would argue that our world is not violent. Crime, war, terrorism, domestic violence, violence against children, and gangs are all part of our culture. What steps can we take for peace despite ever-present violence?

For years, scholars and activists have attempted to find ways to make the world more peaceful. Theories abound. Bookstores offer titles on peacemaking, waging peace, loving others, and stopping war. The issue, however, is more about us than about finding the right system or subscribing to the correct ideology.

? What would it look like if true peace came to your neighborhood?

Until we believe peace is more vital and necessary than conflict and allow ourselves to forgive rather than seek retribution, we will never experience true peace on earth. The biggest roadblock to peace is people. Violence is an easier and faster solution than the painstaking work of peace, so we choose to fight rather than to work it out.

Isaiah brought to his people a new vision of how peace might enter their world. Perhaps his vision can inform our lives too.

Studying

Into another violent land came a peculiar people with new ideas. In that land, only the rich, the powerful, and the well connected enjoyed rights and privileges. Violence was common and inflicted against the vulnerable.

These fresh voices came with a text called Torah, a law that prescribed certain behaviors as beneficial and rejected others as unfit. The Torah insisted that all people were connected to God and had certain rights. According to Torah, the protection of the poor, the outcast, the stranger, and the powerless was a central task of society. The ancient Israelites who believed the words of the Torah found in them a river of life-giving water (Lev 18:5).

Isaiah envisions the Israelites settled in a land where they will live differently than their Canaanite neighbors. Isaiah saw a mountain called Zion, and from this mountain "shall go forth instruction" (v. 3). The imagery of a mountain from which God dispenses instructions for living recalls Israel's experience at Mount Sinai centuries earlier. On that mountain, God gave the original Law to Moses.

Isaiah's vision is also a clear call to a different kind of life. In a violent culture, Isaiah speaks of a time when the way of peace will reign. Although not mentioned in this text, it seems that Isaiah desperately wants a world other than the one Jeremiah (4:23) saw when he proclaimed, "I looked on the earth and lo, it was waste and void." The vision of Mount Zion renews and enlarges the earlier message of Sinai. Rather than imagining peace as a special gift to Israel, Isaiah speaks of God establishing peace throughout the whole world (v. 4).

How can this peace come about? According to Isaiah, it will come when Torah (the Law, God's teaching) becomes the basis on which all people act. Just as the people once came to Sinai to be close to the presence of God, Isaiah envisions a day when the people will come to Zion for the same reason.

In this passage, Zion is a metaphor for the Law. Isaiah is not speaking of a physical hilltop in Jerusalem. Instead, he pictures Torah itself as the mountain of Zion, the place where all people gather so that God "may teach us" and that "we may walk in God's paths" (v. 3). Out of Zion comes instruction that leads to life for all people. Furthermore, this promise is not merely something Isaiah imagines for the far future. It can be a present reality if the people follow the word of God in their lives.

Isaiah's community struggled because the ways of the Canaanites were alive and well among them, even after several centuries of living in the promised land. Isaiah had earlier portrayed much of the temple's worship as bankrupt (1:10-17). Oddly, despite the good news of God's presence, many fell into the trap of believing the stories of the Canaanites more than their own stories of faith. Coercive force often seemed effective as a way to solve problems. At times, violence got them what they wanted, as a cursory reading of Joshua and Judges attests.

In time, the people abandoned God (1:4-17) and went after their hearts' desires, usually at someone else's expense. Anger, envy, jealousy, and greed began to drive the lives of the people. Before they knew it, they were like the Canaanites and had lost much of their resemblance to God. In the end, God looked to the people for signs that they were practicing justice but instead found bloodshed and only pleas for righteousness to come (5:7). It's little wonder that Isaiah urges, "Come let us go up to the mountain of the LORD, to the house of God...let us walk in the light of the LORD!" (vv. 3, 5).

It is tempting to see Isaiah's vision as idealistic, as "pie in the sky." In Isaiah's world and in ours, violence is frequently a given: it is the way we do things. We do not like it or enjoy it, but in the end we know it works.

Or does it? Choosing violence leads us toward chaos. It points us toward a mentality that says the strongest always win. Within that vision, there will come a day when we are not the strongest ones. What will we think of the "myth of redemptive violence" then?

Isaiah's vision is idealistic, but not in the sense of being implausible. If we believe the gospel we proclaim, why are we often shortsighted about God's desire for us to live peacefully— not only in our nation but around the world?

Isaiah offers a portrait of what can be. It is an unfinished picture he intended for his contemporaries, his successors, and now us to continue. Imagine our world pervaded by the vision of peace God taught to Isaiah.

For believers today, the choice is between a vision of Mt. Zion as Isaiah describes it and a vision of the Valley of Armageddon as described in the book of Revelation. Neither vision is set in stone because both depend on us. Our behavior, our choices, and our allegiances determine what finally happens.

Understanding

The film *The Mission* (Warner Brothers, 1986) tells the story of eighteenth-century Jesuit missionaries in northeastern Argentina and western Paraguay. These missionaries, portrayed by Robert DeNiro and Jeremy Irons, find themselves caught in a catch-22 between the Pope in Rome and the colonial authorities of two of Europe's most aggressive powers: the Spanish and the Portuguese. The Jesuit missions in the interior of South America were not popular with the business interests of either power, mostly because the missions provided protection for the indigenous Guaraní, whom the Portuguese colonists coveted as slaves.

The dramatic tension involves the crisis of conscience faced by two very different Jesuits when the Pope's envoy decides to close the mission in favor of Spanish and Portuguese business interests. One missionary, Father Gabriel, has lived his life believing that God is love and that violence in any form denies that love.

The other missionary, Rodrigo Mendoza, came to the mission late in life. Formerly a slave trader and a violent man who even killed his own brother in a fight over a woman, Mendoza has found life and faith inside the mission.

These two must answer the question of whether to fight against the Spanish and Portuguese who are on their way to evict them and the Indians who trust them and to whom they've brought God's love, or to refuse to resort to violence no matter what.

The movie's most significant moments involve scene shifts between Father Gabriel and Mendoza as they make their decisions. Mendoza chooses to stay and fight. Father Gabriel chooses nonviolence. Both are killed by the onslaught of forces against the mission. The movie leaves viewers with an enormous question, because in this scenario neither violence nor nonviolence appears to "win."

Yet perhaps the idea of "winning" is precisely our issue. Isaiah does not envision conflict without fighting, but a people who have changed in such ways that conflict never occurs. His vision is not of peaceful sit-ins or letter campaigns, although either tactic may help in the short term. He sees a vision of a time when the weapons of violence are no longer necessary, except as materials from which to create tools for the care of others.

We keep that vision alive as we learn the words of the Law, the Prophets, and Jesus and seek to embody their message in our lives.

What About Me?

• *Peace is something we do, not a place or a feeling.* Throughout the Bible, peace is an activity, but we may easily assume it is merely a feeling. How can we begin to live out peace in our lives today? How determined are we to live peacefully with others?

• *Education is central to understanding God's intention for us.* The study of Scripture's history, theology, and ethics is decreasing. Fewer people today are biblically literate. The speeches of Abraham Lincoln and Martin Luther King Jr. were laced with references to the Bible. Today, however, many listeners would not recognize those connections. Isaiah also grieved the lack of attention to God's instructions and envisioned the people returning to God's house to learn.

• *Live what you believe!* For those who believe peace is important, it is just as important to act. Unfortunately, we often struggle with time. We are often overwhelmed with our schedules and think we have no time to work for peace. We must make it a priority to find ways to work for peace in our communities, our churches, and our lives.

Resources

Walter Wink, *Engaging the Powers: Discernment and Resistance in a World of Domination* (Minneapolis: Fortress, 1992).

LONGING FOR PEACE

Isaiah 2:1-4

Introduction

Our passage for this week actually occurs twice in the Old Testament. Isaiah 2:1-4 and Micah 4:1-3 are almost word-for-word the same. Most likely, either Micah borrowed from Isaiah or vice-versa. It is also possible that both prophets drew from a third source.

However it happened, both Isaiah and Micah included this poem about all the people coming to the mountain of the Lord in Jerusalem. Once there, these people decide to live in peace. "They beat their swords into plowshares, and their spears into pruning hooks" (Isa 2:4). There, on the mountain with the Lord, "nations shall not lift up sword against nation, neither shall they learn war any more" (Isa 2:4). In the presence of the Lord, Isaiah and Micah say, there will finally be peace.

People have never realized this dream, but it is a dream well worth keeping. We have already seen that the Old Testament is filled with violence and war and that, at times, God is depicted as the instigator. But the Old Testament also offers a recurring prayer for peace. Side by side with mayhem and destruction is the awareness that God is a God of peace. Many parts of the Old Testament, such as our passage this week, anticipate the loving way of Jesus. Those of us who read Isaiah 2 today still find ourselves dreaming of a peaceful world. Like some of our Old Testament forebears, we long for peace and want to do whatever we can to foster it.

In our lesson for this week, we look at Isaiah's old dream and ponder ways we can cooperate with God to make it come true.

Dreaming of Peace

The book of Isaiah spans many years of history: the time before the Babylonian Exile (chs. 1–39), the time during the exile (chs. 40–55), and the time when the exiles came back home (chs. 56–66). The entire book covers a span of about two hundred years and, therefore, was the work of several prophets.

Although the book is obviously the work of more than one writer, a consistent theme of peace runs through the book. The writers of Isaiah all dreamed of peace, of the day when people would lay down their weapons and live in harmony. Our passage in Isaiah 2 is just one example of this consistent longing for peace. Catch the dream of peace in these other passages:

> For all the boots of the tramping warriors and all the garments rolled in blood shall be burned as fuel for the fire. For a child has been born to us, a son given to us; authority rests upon his shoulders; and he is named Wonderful Counselor, Mighty God, Everlasting Father, Prince of Peace. His authority shall grow continually, and there shall be endless peace. (Isa 9:5-7)

> The wolf shall live with the lamb, the leopard shall lie down with the kid, the calf and the lion and the fatling together, and a little child shall lead them. (Isa 11:6)

> Then justice will dwell in the wilderness, and righteousness abide in the fruitful field. The effect of righteousness will be peace, and the result of righteousness, quietness and trust forever. My people will abide in a peaceful habitation, in secure dwellings, and in quiet resting places. (Isa 32:16-18)

> For the mountains may depart and the hills be removed, but my steadfast love shall not depart from you, and my covenant of peace shall not be removed, says the LORD, who has compassion on you. (Isa 54:10)

The writers of Isaiah predicted a day when peace would come and longed for that day, and we join them in that longing. We recognize that war is never God's perfect will and join Isaiah in praying that people will one day beat their swords into plowshares and their spears into pruning hooks.

Surely Jim Wallis is right when he says, "We must stop thinking of war in terms of victory and defeat; rather, war is always a sign of failure—failure of the warring parties to resolve their conflicts in some more peaceful, effective, less costly, and less violent way. War should be a cause, never for celebration, but rather for grief and repentance" (*The Soul of Politics* [New York: Harcourt, 1995] 225).

A Tale of Three Trees

If I had to come up with one word to describe the theme of the Bible, I think I would choose "reconciliation." When we consider the Bible as one long story, we can see why the word "reconciliation" captures the essence of its plot.

The story begins with a tree: the tree of the knowledge of good and evil (Gen 2). Adam and Eve disobey God, sample from this forbidden tree, and are banished from the garden. This tree represents human willfulness, our desire to go our own way, ignoring the commands of God. This tree also represents separation, for Adam and Eve are expelled from the garden and lose communion with God. The first tree in the Bible sets the stage for all that is to come in the story: human beings are separated from God and need to be reconciled.

The story continues, centuries later, with a second tree: the tree on which Jesus died. After centuries of human waywardness and separation, God does something remarkable. God sends Jesus to die on this tree to bridge the gap created back in Genesis. As Paul put it, "All this is from God, who reconciled us to himself through Christ, and has given us the ministry of reconciliation; that is, in Christ God was reconciling the world to himself, not counting their trespasses against them, and entrusting the message of reconciliation to us" (2 Cor 5:18-19). This second tree—call it the tree of reconciliation—was the bridge that made it possible for humans to get back to God.

The story ends with a third tree: the tree of life. Around the tree of life in Revelation, "nothing accursed will be found there any more. But the throne of God and of the Lamb will be in it, and his servants will worship him; they will see his face, and his name will be on their foreheads. And there will be no more night;

they need no light of lamp or sun, for the Lord God will be their light, and they will reign forever and ever" (22:3-5). This third tree gives the biblical story a happy ending. The relationship between God and humans that was intended in the Garden of Eden is restored in Revelation 22. As the curtain falls on the biblical story, reconciliation reigns supreme.

The tree of the knowledge of good and evil is followed by the tree of reconciliation, which makes possible the tree of life. Of course, that is a great over-simplification of the biblical story, but it enables us to glimpse the big picture of reconciliation. Seen from this perspective, the entire Bible is about peace. It shows us the extent to which God will go to bring peace to people. God, as the Bible makes clear, is in the reconciliation business, and those of us who claim to know God are supposed to be in the reconciliation business too. A call to live for God is a call to break down walls.

Some of us grew up saying,

Humpty-Dumpty sat on a wall
Humpty-Dumpty had a great fall
All the king's horses and all the king's men
Couldn't put Humpty together again.

The biblical story dares to say that our Humpty-Dumpty world *can* be put together again. By the end of the story, the sacrifice of Christ has put our fractured, fragmented world back together again. Chaos has become peace because of the cross.

Becoming Peacemakers

How exactly do we become agents of reconciliation? If we are to join the Isaiah 2 Club and bring peace on earth, what do we need to do? More to the point, how do we move beyond *longing* for peace and start *working* for peace? I offer two simple suggestions.

First, we must understand and practice *shalom*. That is the Hebrew word for "peace," the very word Isaiah used to describe his dream. But it means more than merely the absence of conflict. The word literally means "completeness" and has to do with justice and making relationships right. *Shalom* calls us to see ourselves in community. It calls us to get rid of "us and them" distinctions and understand that we are only as strong as the weakest in our world.

Shalom also knows that peace has a lot of connections, that it doesn't exist in a vacuum. When we practice *shalom*, we foster peace by getting rid of the enemies of peace: racism, sexism, materialism, poverty, hunger, loneliness, and exploitation in any form. *Shalom* teaches us that as long as any of those evils exist, peace cannot. *Shalom* prompts us to work for peace by working against the specific conditions that prevent it.

Second, we must grab hold of "the near edge." We must take hold of some evil close at hand and make a difference there. Every time we feed the hungry, we make peace. Every time we build a house for the homeless, we make peace. Every time we reach out to someone who is excluded or exploited, we make peace.

Peacemaking is usually depicted as a political activity done by politicians in a government building somewhere. But peacemaking is actually a personal activity done by ordinary people in a church, school, office, or neighborhood. Peacemaking happens when individual people take on one of those evil peace-killers that is alive and well right where they live.

Colin Morris speaks to this personal aspect of peacemaking when he writes,

> The most that average Christians can hope to do is to take hold of the near edge of a great problem and act at some cost to themselves. The Church is not a Think Group, whose role is to duplicate or supplement the intellectual efforts of others. It is an Action Corps daring to offer simple solutions to complex problems through the creative use of self-sacrifice. (*Include Me Out* [Nashville: Abingdon, 1968], 20-21)

Conclusion

This quotation tells us that the second tree is essential if peace of any kind is going to happen. You can't get from the first tree of the knowledge of good and evil to the third tree of life without the indispensable second tree of reconciliation. Someone must "dare to offer simple solutions to complex problems through the creative use of self-sacrifice," or peace will not occur. That's precisely what Jesus did at the cross, and that's what his followers do, too.

When Jesus invites us to take up our cross daily (Lk 9:23), that's what he has in mind. Just as he had to sacrifice himself to bring about reconciliation with God, so his followers must sacrifice themselves to bring about reconciliation with others. By understanding and embracing the biblical concept of *shalom*, and by grabbing hold of the near edge of some problem close at hand, we do our small part to build a world of peace. We become people of the second tree.

Our little acts of justice and peacemaking may not seem like much, but, according to Jesus himself, our seemingly insignificant actions on behalf of seemingly insignificant people are more important than we know: "Just as you did it to one of the least of these who are members of my family, you did it to me" (Mt 25:40).

Peace is the result of a bunch of "little people" doing a bunch of "little things." Reconciliation happens one tiny act of love at a time.

Notes

Notes

TURNING THE OTHER CHEEK

Luke 6:27-36

Central Question

What does it mean to "turn the other cheek"?

Scripture

Luke 6:27-36 27 "But I say to you that listen, Love your enemies, do good to those who hate you, 28 bless those who curse you, pray for those who abuse you. 29 If anyone strikes you on the cheek, offer the other also; and from anyone who takes away your coat do not withhold even your shirt. 30 Give to everyone who begs from you; and if anyone takes away your goods, do not ask for them again. 31 Do to others as you would have them do to you. 32 If you love those who love you, what credit is that to you? For even sinners love those who love them. 33 If you do good to those who do good to you, what credit is that to you? For even sinners do the same. 34 If you lend to those from whom you hope to receive, what credit is that to you? Even sinners lend to sinners, to receive as much again. 35 But love your enemies, do good, and lend, expecting nothing in return. Your reward will be great, and you will be children of the Most High; for he is kind to the ungrateful and the wicked. 36 Be merciful, just as your Father is merciful."

Reflecting

In the early 1900s, Mohandas K. "Mahatma" Gandhi led India to independence from the oppressive rule of Great Britain. Gandhi provided a means for the Indian people to gain greater freedom and self-determination through nonviolent protest. While working as a lawyer in South Africa, one of his first acts was to hold a public burning of the work passes required of all non-European workers.

Portrayed in the movie *Gandhi* (Columbia Pictures, 1982), the pass-burning scene occurs in the presence of the South African police. After a short speech, one man burns a pass and is arrested. The senior police officer threatens the crowd. As he makes his threat, Gandhi burns several more passes without comment. For this, he receives a violent clubbing across the arm. As Gandhi lies writhing in pain on the ground, the police officer again warns the crowd. He then turns back and sees the injured Gandhi lifting still another pass toward the fire. He strikes Gandhi in the stomach, and Gandhi again collapses. Once again, Gandhi lifts himself and finds the strength to burn still another pass. The policeman becomes enraged and hits Gandhi across the forehead with all his might. Gandhi falls. To his amazement, the policeman sees a set of trembling fingers struggle to grasp still another pass and move it slowly and painfully toward the fire.

At this point, the policeman's demeanor undergoes a profound change. His rage fades and he makes no more demands. Instead of raising his club, the officer—"in charge" only moments ago—now seems desperate. His face contorts

> What do you think caused the policeman to stop beating Gandhi? Can you imagine a situation where Gandhi's nonviolent resistance would have made a police officer even more violent?

with confusion. At this extraordinary moment, control begins to shift from the physically dominant officer to the physically wounded Gandhi. It appears that the policeman's greatest desire is to relent on the threats he so forcefully uttered. He stands almost frozen as another work pass falls into the fire.

Gandhi's fascination with Jesus' teachings led him to focus on nonviolent resistance as a means to win political freedom for his people. He took seriously that the teaching to "turn the other cheek" meant one should never return evil for evil. As he studied the life of Jesus, Gandhi struggled not with believing Jesus' words but with the lack of commitment Christians showed to those words.

Studying

Unlike in Matthew, where Jesus delivers this signature sermon on top of a mountain, in Luke Jesus comes down from the mountain to a level place (6:17). Luke's "Sermon on the Plain" is significantly shorter than Matthew's "Sermon on the Mount" (Matt 5–7). Both sermons reflect back to the Moses event at Sinai (Exod 19:20–23:33). While the two focus on different emphases, Matthew on the "Law and Prophets" and Luke on the ethics of discipleship, both sermons are delivered to the disciples and a nearby crowd.

The background of Jesus' teaching comes from the Old Testament. *Lex talionis* (Latin, "law of retaliation") is a concept in ancient law that allowed for—and in fact demanded—equal and direct retribution. The earliest written code of laws was the Code of Hammurabi, the most famous of the Old Babylonian kings of Mesopotamia. Hammurabi's code of laws was almost entirely based on the principle of equal and direct retribution. Portions of Old Testament law are similar. The best-known version of this idea is the command, "a life for a life, an eye for an eye, a tooth for a tooth, hand for hand, foot for foot, burn for burn, wound for wound" (Ex 21:23–35; Lev 24:20).

Central to this way of thinking was the idea that equal retaliation restored honor. Honor, as we studied in an earlier session, was the most important value in the ancient world. Because it was a limited commodity, the loss of honor was catastrophic to a family. Families worked hard to protect their honor and maintain their standing in the community. Roman law also demanded compensation for a family whose honor was injured not merely physically (in the instance of bodily harm to a family member) but also through insult, which in the eyes of ancient peoples did just as much damage as a physical assault. Even the rabbis of Jesus' day provided for injury to honor: "If a man wounded his fellow he thereby becomes liable on five counts: for injury, for pain, for healing, for loss of time, *and for indignity inflicted*"

(m. Baba Qamma 8:1). "Indignity" referred to one's loss of honor in the community.

Against this idea of preserving one's honor, Jesus offers a contrary teaching. The law commanded Jews to love their neighbors as themselves (Lev 19:18), a teaching Jesus also endorsed. Jesus, however, goes further, because in the context of Leviticus a "neighbor" was merely a person in one's own community, a like-minded friend. In this context, the lawyer asks Jesus, "And who is my neighbor?" (Lk 10:29). He realizes Jesus is working from a different definition. This text urges us not only to love our neighbors but even to love our enemies. Jesus has just told his followers they are blessed when they are hated, excluded, and reviled (6:22). Loving your neighbor is basic. Loving your enemies is difficult for even the most committed. Nevertheless, Scripture provides several examples of Jesus' followers showing concern for their opponents (e.g., Acts 7:58-60; Rom 12:16-21; 1 Thess 5:15; 1 Pet 3:9). Jesus adds to the difficulty here by demanding that his followers bless and pray for those who curse and abuse them.

Jesus offers a few specific examples to help his followers understand what he intends. Clearly, he expects his followers to avoid any kind of retaliation. Instead, we are to respond to our enemies and to those who abuse us with non-defensive behavior. The first example (v. 29) describes an attack on one's honor. In the first-century world, a slap on the face was considered extremely humiliating. Matthew's version of this teaching details which cheek. There, it is clear that the offender either backhands the right cheek (a sign of disregard) or strikes with the left hand to the right side. The left hand was considered unclean because it was always the hand used to care for toiletry needs. Either way, the attack is to one's honor. Jesus asks his disciples to respond by "turning the other cheek." They are not to retaliate in order to regain their honor. Likewise, Jesus describes other scenarios where one's honor is challenged. Each time, whether in a legal dispute, a situation of need, or even robbery, Jesus opposes violent retaliation.

Jesus goes on to describe how his followers can choose a different kind of honor, based not on stature within the community but on love. In that day, providing basic food, water, and shelter for travelers was a cultural expectation based on ancient codes of hospitality. At the same time, families and communities tended to care for their own, effectively loving those who loved them back. Jesus challenges this system. Even sinners, he says, can love those who love them. Jesus asks more. Love those who are not your friends, your neighbors, or your relatives—love your enemies as if they were your friends, neighbors, or relatives. Turning the other cheek is not a command to get hit twice, although that may happen. It is a call to change the way the world works and the way we look at one another.

Understanding

Turning the other cheek is not a call to accept a beating. There is a difference between pacifism and passivism. Passivism is doing nothing; it is standing in the face of violence and becoming a victim. Pacifism is a call to work against violence and find other ways to respond. While Gandhi was abused as a result of his stand, he refused to stop taking a stand, and eventually, at least as portrayed in the movie, his attacker relented.

Far too often, we assume that the only way to respond to violence is with violence. There are at least two problems with this assumption. First, there is no evidence that using violence against violence actually works. Instead, escalation or revenge are the usual results. Second, it is not the case that choosing pacifism makes one a coward. In fact, it takes incredible courage to stand one's ground and refuse to use violence at the same time.

A frequent problem is the "worst-case scenario." We wonder, "What happens if...?" It is helpful to ask these kinds of questions because they force us to look at ourselves and what we do to promote peace. All relationships take work. In order to find peace, to understand fully what Jesus meant by encouraging us to "turn the other cheek," we must consider our responsibility in waging peace.

In a culture where violence has become an acceptable norm, what actions are congregations and individuals taking to promote peaceful relationships? Are we willing to settle for needing more bombs, more military, more police, more metal detectors, and more fences in order to keep the violence out of our lives, neighborhoods, and world? Or are we willing to take the more courageous steps of choosing to begin the hard work of waging peace, not only for ourselves but for all of God's world?

In our context, what is similar to turning the other cheek? What is a way for us to change how we look at our relationships and deal with enemies, conflict, and violence? First, standing against violence in the media is a good place to start. Television and music both play an integral role in the lives of young people. Refusing to purchase or watch violence is a form of protest that works, especially if you encourage others to join you. Second, learn new ways to resolve conflict. We have done a poor job of teaching young people how to deal with conflict in a productive way. Third, work for and demand justice in your community. Fourth, develop deeper and more diverse relationships in your community. Fifth, learn to listen to those who are different from you. Always ask yourself before forming an opinion about others, "What is the truth in what this person says?"

It is possible for us to live the ethic Jesus demands. Probably the greatest disservice we do to Jesus' teachings is to treat them like Grandmother's china—worth keeping but too much trouble to use.

What About Me?

• *Consider the role you play in allowing violence in the world.* A proverbial saying goes, "In every avalanche, the individual snowflakes plead 'Not guilty!'" We do not need to bear the burden of every conflict, but it is unfair for us to expect peace in our lives or in the world and then do nothing to promote it.

• *Practice being the kind of person you want to become.* Jesus knew his followers would fail. He offers us the guidance of the Spirit, the encouragement of hope, and the power of grace to help us become who we are called to be. At the same time, we also have a responsibility to practice what we say we believe. How can we expect to handle a major conflict if we have not practiced our faith in smaller ones?

• *Do what the Bible says.* Love your neighbor. Pray for your enemies. Bless those who persecute you. Forgive. It will take us a lifetime to learn these four, but in the process we will be changed and make a vast difference in the world around us.

Resources

Richard B. Vinson, *Luke*, Smyth & Helwys Bible Commentary (Macon GA: Smyth & Helwys, 2008).

TURNING THE OTHER CHEEK

Luke 6:27-36

Introduction

Recently a pilot was practicing high-speed maneuvers in a jet fighter. She turned the controls for what she thought was a steep ascent—and flew straight into the ground. She was unaware that she had been flying upside down.

This is a parable of human existence in our times—not exactly that everyone is crashing, though there is enough of that—but most of us as individuals, and world society as a whole, live at high-speed, and often with no clue to whether we are flying upside down or right-side up. (Dallas Willard, *The Divine Conspiracy* [San Francisco: HarperCollins, 1998] 1–2)

If our verses for this week seem strange and even impossible to us, it is probably because our culture has been flying upside down for a long time. Jesus' words in Luke 6 introduce us to a strange world where people love their enemies, do good to those who hate them, bless those who curse them, and pray for those who abuse them. It seems like a bizarre, unbelievable world because it is a world flying right-side up, and we've seldom if ever experienced such a world.

One way to think of the life and ministry of Jesus is like this: he came to show us what a right-side up world looks like. He called this new world "the kingdom of God" and made it the centerpiece of his teachings.

In our passage for this week, Jesus shows that living in the kingdom of God means living by a new ethic and before a new audience. If we're ever going to fly right-side up, we'll have to find this new ethic and this new audience.

A New Ethic

What exactly does it mean to live in the kingdom of God and fly right-side up? It means we take passages like Luke 6 seriously and love our enemies, do good to those who hate us, bless those who curse us, and pray for those who abuse us. Easier said than done, don't you think? The Jesus way is not for the faint of heart! It makes an ethical demand of us that seems impossible to follow.

Then, just to make sure we understand, Jesus gets even more specific about his way of life in verses 29-31. If someone strikes us on the cheek, he says, we are to offer the other cheek also. If someone takes our coat, we should offer that person our shirt as well. If someone begs from us, we should give to that person gladly. If someone "rips us off" and steals our goods, we should not try to get those goods back. We should treat every person the way we would like to be treated. It seems so bizarre and unfair that we shake our heads in amazement when we read these things. If Jesus is anywhere near the truth, then we are truly living upside down.

I offer you three simple observations about this new ethic Jesus describes:

First, *this new ethic is the only hope for peace in the world.* These responses are important because they break the cycle of violence, anger, and hostility. As long as I hit you back, get mad at you, and respond to you in kind, there is no hope for peace. The downward cycle of hostility will go on forever—an eye for an eye and a tooth for a tooth until all of us can only stumble around in the dark gumming our food. This cycle can be turned around only by someone's gracious response, and Jesus says that someone should be the people who know him. He eventually let himself be nailed to a cross and died between two thieves to show us precisely what he meant.

Second, *this new ethic is built on a series of positive actions.* Many of us grew up with the idea that Christianity is a set of prohibitions: don't drink, don't smoke, don't dance, don't play cards, and so on and so on. The Jesus way, we came to believe, is a road filled with angry warning signs. But Luke 6 offers another perspective. The Jesus way is a way of positive actions. It is not a way of prohibitions; it is a way of turning the other cheek, offering our shirt, giving freely, and seeking reconciliation. In light of Luke 6, we can justifiably toss out the notion of the Christian life as a somber, gray, or negative way to live. It is a risking, gambling, positive journey. It is daring to fly right-side up in an upside-down world.

Third, *this new ethic centers on the practical and "ordinary."* Someday, we think, we will do something big for God. We will surrender our life and become a missionary to Africa. We will become a famous preacher and hold crusades around the world. Or perhaps we will strike it rich and give millions of dollars to life-changing ministry causes. Those things might happen to some of us, but not to most of us. Most of us will live out our faith precisely where Jesus says we will—in our relationships, in the ordinary nitty-gritty details of life. If peace touches in our lives, and our world, it will be because we are faithful to Jesus in practical, ordinary ways—turning cheeks, giving shirts, offering money to beggars, and not seeking vengeance when we are mistreated. Jesus in Luke 6 gets down to where we live and tells us how to behave.

A New Audience

One of the oldest games in human history is "Keeping Up with the Joneses." We all tend to take our cues from the people around us and try to measure up to their standards. If the Joneses get a new swimming pool, we think we need one, too. If the Joneses go on a cruise to Hawaii, we decide to do the same. And if the Joneses don't like the people of a different race or ethnicity who moved into the neighborhood, we don't like them either. It is fair to say that most of us get our ethics, motivation, and goals from our society. In short, our audience is the world. We live before an audience of many and try to step to their beat.

When our children were small, they occasionally flirted with mischief and then used as their excuse, "Well, Frankie and Suzie did it." Our response was the typical parental one in such a situation: "If Frankie and Suzie jumped off a roof or robbed a bank, would you do that, too?" It was a good question, but, truthfully, we adults are no better than children when it comes to why we do things. Even as adults, we take our cues from Frankie and Suzie.

Whether or not we like to admit it, the mindless attitude of "monkey see, monkey do" still reigns in our world. We all tend to fall in step with the people around us.

But in Luke 6, Jesus calls that tendency into question. He says if we love those who love us, what credit is that to us? If we do good to those who do good to us, why should we boast about that? If we lend money to those who are guaranteed to pay us back, where's the virtue in that? In other words, if we do what everyone else is already doing, how does that show love to anyone? If we live before the audience of the world according to the world's standards, we're no different from those who don't know God. Even people flying upside down do those things.

Instead, Jesus calls us to live before an audience of One: "But love your enemies, do good, and lend, expecting nothing in return. Your reward will be great, and you will be children of the Most High; for he is kind to the ungrateful and the wicked. Be merciful, just as your Father is merciful" (Lk 6:35-36). According to Jesus, his people don't take their cues from the world at all; they take their cues from a merciful Father who sends rain on the just and the unjust and is madly in love with prodigals and sinners. Flying right-side up calls us to know and emulate God.

Søren Kierkegaard, the Danish philosopher, once gave an illustration about worship that speaks to this new audience before whom we are to live. If we think of worship as a drama with actors, prompters, and an audience, Kierkegaard said, we usually assign the roles wrongly. He said we usually think of the actors in worship as the worship leaders—on stage singing, praying, preaching, and leading the people to experience God. He said we typically think of the prompter as God—off stage whispering inspiration and revelation to the worship leaders. And, Kierkegaard said, we think of the audience as the worshipers—gathered to watch the actors play their roles and hoping they will perform well enough to enable the worshipers to see and hear God.

But the roles should be assigned differently, Kierkegaard believed. In true worship, the actors are the worshipers—offering themselves to God, singing and praying and giving with joy. The prompters are the worship leaders—enabling the actors/worshipers to play their roles better. And the audience is God—listening and watching as the worshipers play their roles. Everything done in real worship, Kierkegaard believed, is done before an audience of One.

What Kierkegaard said of worship is true for all of life. According to Jesus, we lead our entire lives before an audience of One. We live before God. We get our motivation from God. We take our cues from God. We receive the incredible grace of God and then dare to give grace away in tangible ways: turning our cheek, offering our coat, giving to beggars, and not hoarding our possessions.

For the follower of Jesus, "Keeping Up With the Joneses" is replaced by "Learning to Love like God."

Conclusion

In *The Divine Conspiracy*, Dallas Willard calls the way of Jesus "the great inversion." In the Gospels, Jesus consistently takes human assumptions and inverts them, turns them upside down. It is safe to say that his way is only for nonconformists and those willing to walk a narrow road.

These verses from Luke 6 are a prime example of the great inversion. Common sense dictates that we dislike our enemies, take a stand against those who hate us, curse those who curse us, and strike back at those who abuse us. That seems sensible and expected. But Jesus inverts those truths and tells us to love our enemies, do good to those who hate us, bless those who curse us, and pray for those who abuse us. That seems insensible and unexpected! But it's the way of Jesus. His followers live by a new ethic before a new audience, and they are peculiar people indeed.

There is one more thing to notice about these verses. In verse 27, Jesus introduces the great inversion this way: "But I say to you who listen...." The implication is that not everyone will have ears to hear what he says. Only those who listen will "get it."

Suffice it to say that Luke 6:27-36 will not be everybody's cup of tea. Some people will never even read this passage. Some will read it and dismiss it as the impossible teachings of an impractical dreamer. Some will read it, claim to believe it, and then continue to live under the old ethic before the old audience.

But some will read it, take Jesus seriously, and look for ways to be radically different than their neighbors. They will do small, practical, nonconforming things that, at least for a brief moment, cause the world around them to fly right-side up.

Notes

Notes

1 Peter
Keep Hope Alive

This study of First Peter focuses on keeping hope alive in the face of pressures and circumstances that could possibly extinguish it completely, or worse, turn authentic faith into a pale replica of the real thing.

Advent Virtues

The phrase "holiday rush" is not an exaggeration. The frantic pace required to purchase gifts, bake holiday foods, and attend Christmas parties, plays, and performances takes its toll; we arrive at Christmas Day exhausted. Within the context of December busyness, the ancient Christian season of Advent takes on new meaning and acquires renewed importance. May God instill the virtues of *hope*, *peace*, *joy*, *love*, and *faith* in each of us this Advent.

Apocalyptic Literature

This study examines five apocalyptic texts in the Bible—from Zechariah, Daniel, Matthew, and Revelation. With each new year bringing a new prediction of impending doom, it is always a perfect time to get the story straight. Apocalyptic literature does not address the future. It addresses our present.

Approaching a Missional Mindset

The World isn't the same as it once was. We must be the church in a new place, in unimagined ways, and with a wider range of people. Engage your small group with the radical and refreshing challenge of developing a "missional lifestyle."

To order call **800-747-3016** or visit **www.nextsunday.com**

Baptist Freedom
Celebrating Our Baptist Heritage

What makes a Baptist a Baptist? Of course, the ultimate answer is simple: membership in a local Baptist church. But there are all kinds of Baptist churches! What are the spiritual and theological marks of a Baptist? What is the shape and the feel of Baptist Christianity?

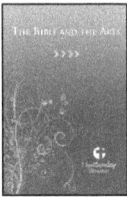

The Bible and the Arts

God has used artistic expression throughout the centuries to convey truth, offer blessing, and urge believers to deeper faithfulness. In modern life, artistic expression flourishes, from movies to books to music to paintings to photographs. Sometimes artists are intentional about trying to portray God's truths. Other times, perhaps God is working even when the artist is unaware of it. As believers, we may hear and see God at work in many art forms.

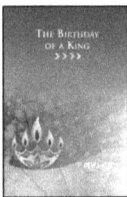

The Birthday of a King

The first four lessons in this unit draw inspiration from a traditional interpretation of the Advent candles as the Prophets' Candle, the Bethlehem Candle, the Shepherds' Candle, and the Angels' Candle. The final lesson, which occurs after Advent, celebrates the theological meaning of Jesus' birth as described in the prologue to John's Gospel.

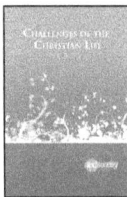

Challenges of the Christian Life

The way of the cross is difficult, and taking Jesus seriously means looking honestly at how we fall short of God's best hopes for us and seeing how much we need God's grace. For all of us there are times when we need to remember that Christ is our saving grace and recommit ourselves to the journey of faith, rediscovering, again and again, the life-giving purpose described in the book of Ephesians.

Christ Is Born!

Even in the midst of difficult circumstances, Advent is a time when we can find hope. Much like today, people in the 1st century church faced struggles. Examining the Gospel of Matthew, lessons include "Waiting for Christ," "Preparing for Christ," "Expecting Christ," "Announcing Christ," and "The Arrival of Christ."

Christians and Hunger

These sessions challenge us to apply gospel lenses and holy imagination to what literally gives us energy to live: food. With God's grace, we have the opportunity to imagine communities where tables are large and all are fed.

Christians and the Public Square

Politics and faith are tricky areas for Christians to negotiate. The First Amendment to the Constitution guarantees religious freedom for all Americans. As Christians who are also citizens, questions abound: How do we distinguish between faithful and unfaithful forms of civic engagement? How do we give Caesar his due while giving our all to God?

Christmas in Mark

In the early chapters of Mark, we will encounter a Christmas story. This story, however, will not be quite like the one told by other Gospel writers, but it will resonate with the reality of your life. Mark doesn't deny the beauty or reality of the nativity; however, he seems to believe that Christmas begins—the gospel begins— when Christ intrudes upon the hard realities of life.

The Church on a Mission

What does it mean to be a church on a mission? The lesson of Acts 1:8 is that we must simultaneously carry out Christ's mandate at home, in our region, in places that have been our blind spots, and around the world.

Colossians
Living the Faith Faithfully

Paul's letter to the Colossians begins with a high-minded philosophical defense of the faith, but concludes with a collection of extremely practical advice for living by faith. This study addresses the questions many Christians face today, helping them apply Paul's practical advice in their own lives.

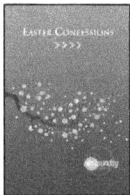

Easter Confessions

Easter confession is often found on many different lips in the Gospel of John. When we listen carefully, those ancient confessions still echo into this new millennium.

Embracing the Word of God

We live during a time of transition in Christian history. Basic assumptions about the truth of the Christian faith are being questioned, not only by nonbelievers, but by Christians themselves. First John offers a starting point for understanding of what it means to "be" Christian.

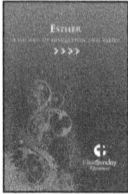

Esther: A Woman of Discretion and Valor

The book of Esther is not a record of historical facts as such. Rather, it is a magnificent narrative that refuses to interpret life as being driven by coincidence or happenstance. In the otherwise unknown characters of Esther, Haman, and Mordecai, we trace the movement of the divine hand as God collaborates with God's risk-taking people to rescue them from the hand of their enemies.

Facing Life's Challenges

This study explores four significant challenges common to most persons of faith: the challenge of new light, the challenge of time's limit, the challenge of living with mystery, and the challenge of authentic spirituality. Although these issues are neither simple nor easy to ponder, this study effectively leads us in confronting these challenges.

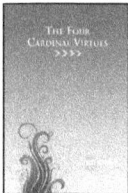

The Four Cardinal Virtues

Christians are learning how to distinguish between members of a church and disciples of Christ. Discipleship involves developing virtues in those who come to our churches seeking life, salvation, grace, mercy. If we want to have something to offer a world in desperate need, then we must return to virtues like discernment, justice, courage, and moderation. We must return to the hard and glorious work of making disciples.

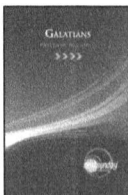

Galatians
Freedom in Christ

Paul wrote with fiery passion, as you will notice from the opening paragraphs of this letter to the Galatians. But his language reveals that he was writing about a crucially important issue—the very nature of salvation in Christ.

A Holy and Surprising Birth

Christmas begins here—discover these five love stories from the book of Luke and renew your appreciation of God's laborious effort to birth our salvation.

How Does the Church Decide?

An array of decisions draw energy and time from church members. These decisions may be theological, such as mode of baptism, aesthetic, such as the color of the sanctuary carpet, or functional, such as the selection of a new minister. This study will consider how the church has made its decisions in the past to help guide our decisions today.

Is God Calling?

Witness the varying forms of God's call, the variety of people called, and the variety of responses. Perhaps God's call to you will become clearer.

James
Gaining True Wisdom

If we'll be honest with God and ourselves as we study what James says, we can make great strides toward wisdom and a living faith.

Life Lessons from Bathsheba

Who was Bathsheba? She was a complex figure who developed from the silent object of David's lust into a powerful, vocal, and influential queen mother.

Life Lessons from David

In the Bible, we catch David in the various stages of the human journey: childhood, adolescence, adulthood, and senior adulthood. From the biblical treatment of the stages of David's life, we can land some insights to assist us in better understanding the human journey.

The Matriarchs

The matriarchs of Genesis offer their lives as a testimony of faith, perseverance, and audacity. We learn from their mistakes and suffering. We will gain the hope of Hagar, the joy of Sarah, and the audacity of Rebekah as we are challenged to examine our prejudices and our insecurities while studying Esau and Jacob's wives.

Missional Hospitality

If we are serious about following Jesus, we will be people of open hearts, open hands, and open homes. In other words, as followers of Jesus we will practice the fine art of hospitality. In lesson one, we reflect on hospitality to strangers. In lesson two, we address hospitality to the poor. In lesson three, we focus on hospitality to sinners. In lesson four, we learn about hospitality to newcomers. Lesson five reminds us about our hospitality to Christ.

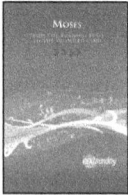

Moses
From the Burning Bush to the Promised Land

We would do well to trace the life of Moses so we might discover how his life changed, both personally and as Israel's leader, as he learned what it meant to love God with all his heart, soul, and strength.

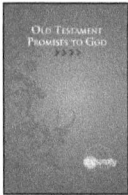

Old Testament Promises to God

Some individuals may feel that our promises couldn't possibly mean anything to God. Perhaps the real question is this: under what circumstances should or do we make such promises? The Old Testament contains several examples of people making promises to God, using the unique form of a biblical "vow."

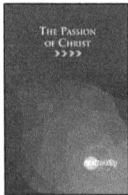

The Passion of Christ

The four lessons in this unit highlight the faith struggles of the early disciples. In lesson one, Jesus addresses the issues of faith and practice. In lesson two, we meet Judas who, like us, struggled with God's Kingdom and human kingdoms. In lesson three, the issue of temptation reminds us that our faith journey is a constant challenge. Lesson Four invites us to remember Peter's experience of "faith failure." Peter's failure, however, is not the final word. There is forgiveness.

The Prayer Life of Jesus

The study of Jesus' prayer life can deepen our own prayer practices. These five sessions examine the importance of prayer at various stages of Jesus' life and ministry. He made no important decisions without consulting God.

Proverbs for Living

Long ago, a collection of wise teachers committed themselves to the ways of God and collected this wisdom into what we know as the book of Proverbs. These four lessons explore the simple truth of Proverbs: there is a good life to be had—a life lived in faithfulness to God.

Qualities of Our Missional God

Too often we are tempted to let "numbers" drive missions. The book of Numbers reminds us that missions is motivated by something deeper. Missions reflects the heart and nature of God. If we can just get past the math, we can see God's nature clearly in the book of Numbers. . . in the wilderness.

The Seven Deadly Sins

What exactly is sin? Just as we organize our cupboards and our schedules to make sense of our lives, Christian thinkers have organized sin into a number of categories in order to understand and surrender these patterns to God. The notion of "seven deadly sins" emerged as a way to recognize specific dangers to our spiritual lives. The purpose of the book is to guide people away from sin and into a wise and godly life.

Seeking Holiness in the Sermon on the Mount

The Sermon on the Mount has long been recognized as the pinnacle of Jesus' teaching. But with this importance in mind, it's easy to think of Jesus' teachings as lofty and idealistic, offering little guidance for everyday life. Perhaps Jesus' sermon allows us to see beyond ourselves, beyond our own failures and shortcomings— revealing God's intention for our lives.

Spiritual Disciplines
Obligation or Opportunity?

The spiritual disciplines help deepen a believer's faith and increases his or her intimacy with Christ. In this study, we take a deeper look at some of the disciplines and consider their practice as a response to God's love.

Stewardship
A Way of Living

Great News! Stewardship is not about money! At least not *just* about money. Certainly, stewardship relates to money, and, yes, we need to tithe. However, stewardship branches out into multiple areas of life. Properly practiced, this act of service can lead to peace and purpose in living.

The Ten Commandments

When the Ten Commandments are in the news, it is usually because a judge or teacher has hung them up on the walls. The Ten Commandments do not need to be posted or even preached nearly so much as they need to be practiced and viewed as life-giving, joyful affirmations of a better way of life.

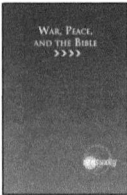

War, Peace, and the Bible

As people of faith, we are faced daily with an expectation that we participate in violent actions, our willingness to allow violence in the world to continue, and our response to violence in our lives. Is there a place for war and violence in our faith?

What Would Jesus Say?
A Lenten Study

To address what Jesus would say, we need to discover what Jesus did say. These lessons will attempt to help us understand Jesus' teachings and apply them today.

www.ingramcontent.com/pod-product-compliance
Lightning Source LLC
Chambersburg PA
CBHW060656030426
42337CB00017B/2648